Killer Technique® Classical Guitar

by Gohar Vardanyan

1 2

Visit us on the Web at www.melbay.com — E-mail us at email@melbay.com

Table of Contents

Killer Technique® Classical Guitar

Introduction

Working on our technique is one of the most important investments we can make into our playing. Having great technique enables us to play music the way it was meant to be instead of the way our technique dictates us. The best technique should be completely invisible, in order for the music to shine through without any hindrance from our physical abilities as players. In addition to the regular practice of scales, arpeggios, slurs, tremolo, etc, we should also do targeted exercises for different challenges in our playing. After playing the guitar for twenty five years, I have discovered that there are certain elements that affect all of our playing, no matter how technically advanced we might be.

Instead of just making up exercises, all the exercises in this book are either based on or inspired by challenging passages and patterns that appear in regular pieces. The technical elements or passages have been stripped down and adapted into exercises in order to allow concentration on a specific target and repetition of that target. Think of them as your vocabulary for the language that is guitar repertoire. The exercises include a number of different areas, such as finger independence in both hands, different types of shifts, in-context slurs, in-context arpeggios and scales, and tremolo.

You will notice that unlike the other guitar books in the Killer Technique series, this book uses standard notation and tablature for the exercises. After giving it a lot of thought, I decided that in classical guitar there are too many detailed indications for fingering in both hands and writing in anything but standard notation would actually complicate the reading process. By using standard notation, the details are presented more clearly. All exercises are also provided in tablature, however the rhythm and finger information is written on the standard staff.

The following exercises are divided into two main sections: Right-Hand and Left-Hand. Each section consists of different categories specific to that hand. The different exercises are not written in any particular order within each category. These are some of the most common difficulties that arise in repertoire. By isolating them into exercises, we can better master the difficulty and be better prepared when they are encountered in the context of our pieces. This by no means is a comprehensive list; there is an endless variety of exercises that we can do. After going through the exercises in this book go through your own repertoire and isolate any section, passage, or element that is the most difficult for you. Break it down to the smallest component, even down to just two or three notes, and create an exercise to target and concentrate on that specific spot. If the difficulty is in the right hand, eliminate the left hand to concentrate on the challenge.

RIGHT HAND WORKOUT

General Instructions:

- Always use a metronome to guide you.
- With each exercise start out slowly enough so you can understand the challenge and execute it perfectly.
- Pay attention to the quality of sound; just because it is an exercise doesn't mean you should accept poor sound quality.
- Most of the right hand exercises are written on open strings to target the right pattern and to not allow distraction from the left hand. You can add chords as you please if you get tired of the open string sound.
- Some of the exercises have suggested starting tempos, to give you an idea of how slowly you should start.

Arpeggios

Exercise 1:

Repeat each measure as many times as necessary. Move same exercise to strings 2 & 3, 3 & 4, 4 & 5, 5 & 6.

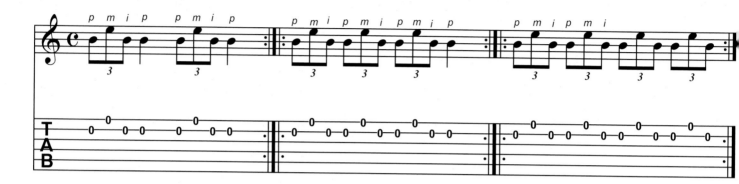

Exercise 2:

This is the same right hand pattern as above, but with string crossings. Pay attention to the *p* finger when playing the 2nd string, after *i* plays the 3rd string. Make sure *p* is always accurate. Move same exercise to strings 2 & 3, 3 & 4, 4 & 5, 5 & 6.

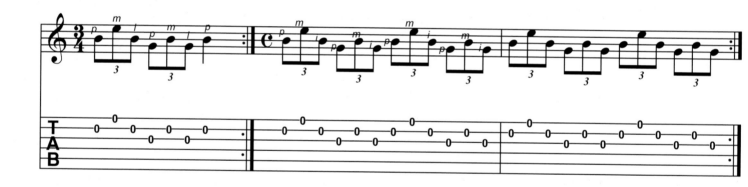

Exercise 3:

A similar arpeggio pattern will be played with different fingering, when presented in different context.

Exercise 3: Reverse order

Exercise 4:

This is one of the most common finger combinations for this kind of arpeggio pattern. Like in the previous exercises you can change which 4 strings you use to do the pattern.

Exercise 5:

To add context to the above pattern, play it with the left hand. Make sure all the chromatic shifts are clear and accurate in both hands. Move it up to the middle four strings and lower four strings.

Often we come across an arpeggio that has more notes than we have fingers. The smoothest fingering for these forces us to double/triple-stroke the p and drag the *a* (or *i*) finger across multiple strings. These harp like arpeggios are some of the most beautiful, but when played on the guitar, they often sound uneven and broken into two sections – ascending and descending. Practicing them while subdividing with the metronome will help place all the notes in correct time, even when dragging one finger across multiple strings.

This is one of the ways the arpeggio might appear in repertoire. It might also appear starting with the highest string first, i.e. 1st string down to 6th, back up to 1st.

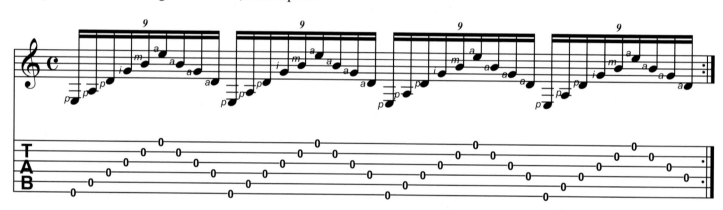

Instead of practicing in groups of 9, subdivide into different divisions of the beat, even if that means displacing the beat from the first note of the pattern by placing it into duple divisions. If the arpeggio in your piece is written in a 10-note pattern, then the triplet subdivision will displace the beat. Start slow enough to control each individual note, even when dragging the *a* finger. There should be no difference in time or sound quality when switching between the right hand fingers.

Exercise 6a: Triplet division
Suggested starting tempo: ♩ = 50

Exercise 6b: Duple division
Suggested starting tempo: ♩ = 70

Exercise 6c: Quadruple division
Suggested starting tempo: ♩ = 40

Though the *a* finger is the most common choice, some people choose to drag the *i* finger, as shown below.

Arpeggio to Rest Stroke Alternation

Practicing scales and arpeggios on their own is a great way to improve them individually. However, when we play a piece of music we often need to seamlessly switch between one and the other. Free stroke scales are easier to play between arpeggios, since the basics of the stroke don't change between the arpeggio and free stroke scales. The following exercise is intended for practicing arpeggio and **rest stroke** scale combinations. In order to successfully play this exercise, it is important to maintain a uniform right hand position between the rest stroke scale and the arpeggio, to easily switch between the two techniques.

*The small arrow markings pointing up indicate rest stroke.

Exercise 1: Arpeggio to Rest Stroke Scales

Exercise 2:

Put it together into context by adding the left hand.

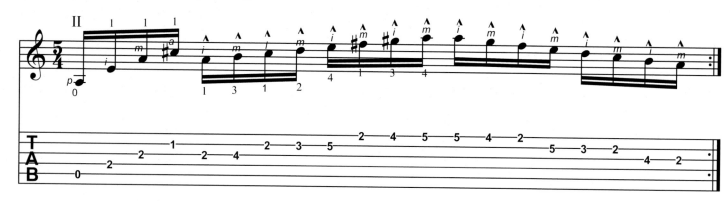

Continue going up the fingerboard.

To isolate the switch between strokes, play just the first two notes of the scale until you are comfortable with it.

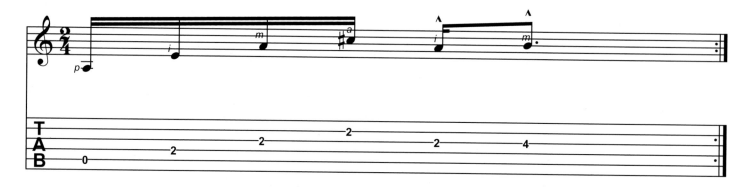

Chord and Scale

In the previous exercises of arpeggio and scales, your *i* finger had time to get to the first note of the scale, because it wasn't the last finger to play in the arpeggio. When playing blocked chords, that time is no longer there and your *i* (or *m*) has to be very quick to pluck the next note. Once again, you can choose to play the notes free stroke in your pieces; however some passages in music ask for rest stroke to follow a blocked chord. The point is to be fluent in all of the technical vocabulary, and not have any limitations.

Exercise 1:

If the music asks for the chord to be strummed with the thumb, then we need to train our hand to get back into position quickly enough to continue playing the passage in time. The farther the first note of the scale is, e.g. on the 3rd string, the more difficult it is to play it accurately, securely, and in time. Try not to move your hand too far down when rolling down the *p*, so you can quickly get back.

Exercise 2:

P and *I* Alternations

Often we have to play two individual lines with our right hand. The problem is, we only have 4 fingers. Training the *p* and *i* to work seamlessly together will give us more options when fingering the right hand.

You can start with a simple open string exercise for the *p* and *i* alternations. Make sure you control the sound for both fingers, so they are as similar to each other as possible.

Exercise 1: *p* and *i*

Exercise 2: *p*, *i* and *a*

Once you're comfortable with the previous, add the *a* finger as a second line.

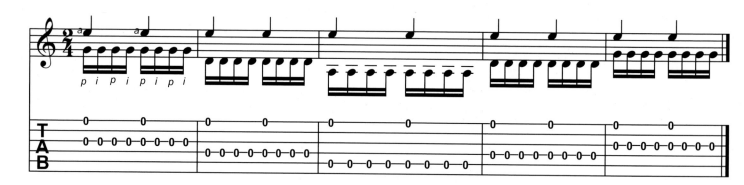

Exercise 3: *p*, *i* and *a* in context

When it comes to real repertoire, you will most often find this kind of pattern with different string combinations. Make sure the *p* and *i* are even, with uniform sound, and well balanced with the *a*.

Tremolo

For the best tremolo, it isn't enough just to play the regular pattern of *p*, *a*, *m*, *i*. In order to have even tremolo we have to diversify and train individual finger pairings to be strong and independent of each other.

Here are some variations you can use when you practice your tremolo pieces. The exercise is written on open strings with a non particular bass pattern. You can choose whatever bass pattern you prefer, as long as you get a combination of all strings. This will allow your right hand to practice with various spacing between the bass and the tremolo strings.

Exercise 1:

Exercise 2:

Exercise 3:

Exercise 4:

Exercise 5:

To add another level of training, practice the regular *p*, *a*, *m*, *i* pattern and change the location of the metronome beat by starting on a different note of the pattern.

Exercise 6:

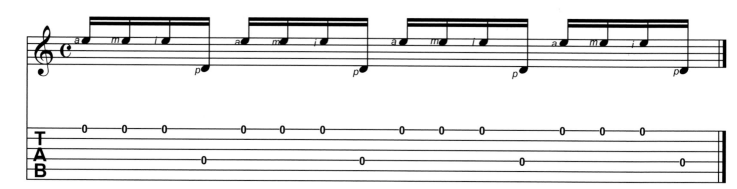

Exercise 7:

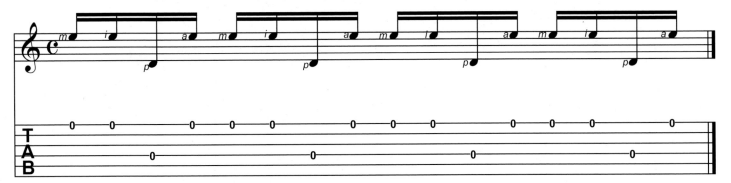

Exercise 8:

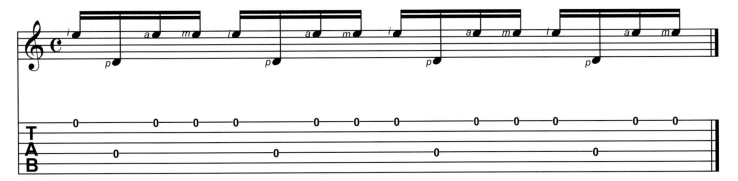

LEFT HAND WORKOUT

General Instructions:

- Always use a metronome to guide you.
- With each exercise start out slowly enough, so you can understand the challenge and execute it perfectly.
- Make sure that the left hand is always in proper position and isn't moving side to side when shifting.
- For some exercises, only the initial repetitions are written out. Continue in the set manner until you've covered all the frets on the fret board.

Shifting

On a perfect instrument, a chromatic scale on one string wouldn't automatically be phrased according to the fingering used. In order to even it out, practice the chromatic scale with the metronome and place the metronome beats on different fingers in the sequence, so that the notes are grouped independently from the finger patterns. The exercises are written on the 3rd string as an example. You can play them on any desired string. The point of the exercise is to make the shifts as seamless as possible, so that the fingering doesn't introduce its own phrasing.

Exercise 1:

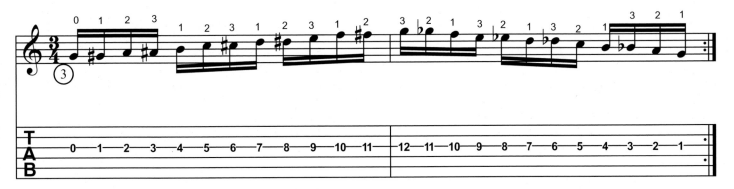

Exercise 2:

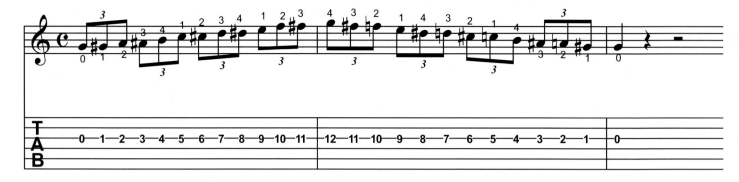

Often in pieces we need to shift and switch fingers at the same time to set up for the fingering that follows the shift. The variations of the following exercise isolate two finger combinations at a time. Pay careful attention to the fingering that is indicated. Though the exercise is written to start on the 4th fret of the 3rd string, you can move it to any string or position.

Exercise 3: Adjacent frets

In order to maximize the switch/shift vocabulary, extend the exercise to all finger pairings, e.g. 3 & 2, 4 & 3, 3 & 1, 4 & 2.

Exercise 3a:

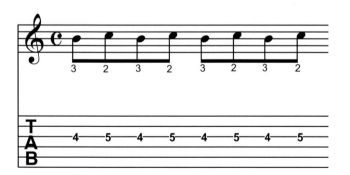

Exercise 3b:

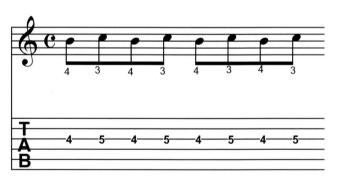

Exercise 3c:

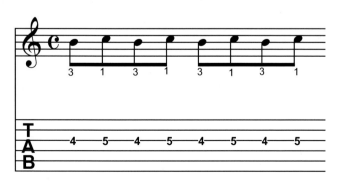

Exercise 3d:

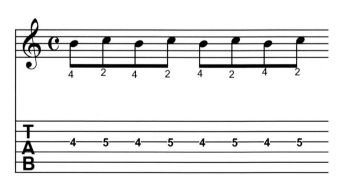

14

Exercise 4: Skipping frets

After mastering the shift on adjacent frets, increase the shift by one fret at a time. The following exercise is written with fingers 2 & 1, just like in the previous versions; use all the fingering pairings, 3 & 2, 4 & 3, 3 & 1, 4 & 2.

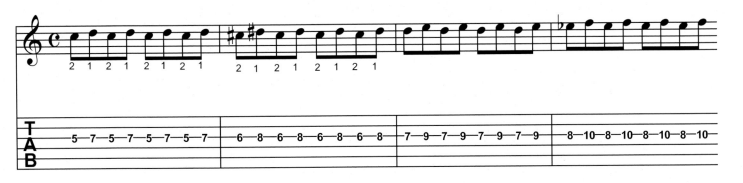

Exercise 4a:

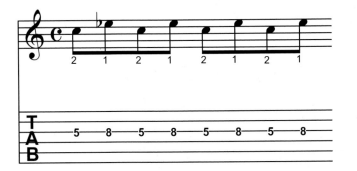

Exercise 4b:

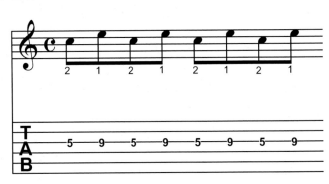

Continue increasing the number of frets between shifts.

Finger Independence

When we need to play a fast passage, especially in a scalier form, there are different things that can slow us down. When it comes to the left hand, lack of independence between the 2nd and 3rd (also 3rd and 4th) fingers is one of the first culprits. At first the following exercises might seem easy, but as the tempo is increased, you will notice the weakness between the targeted fingers begins to show.

Only the initial shifts are written out; continue shifting down until you reach first position. For exercises 1 and 2, I like to start in the middle of the fret board, move all the way down to 1st position, then up to 10th position and back to the middle. You can start in 10th, or in 1st.

*NOTE: positions are determined by the location of the 1st finger, so 10th position would have the 3rd finger on the 12th fret.

Exercise 1: Fingers 2 – 3

15

Exercise 2: Fingers 3 – 2

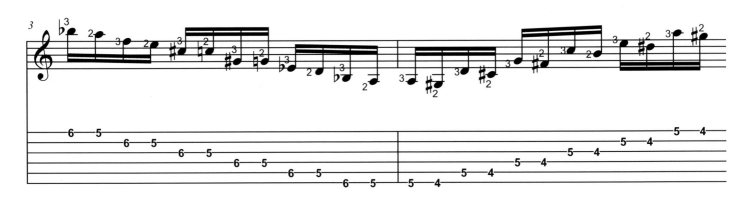

Exercise 3: Fingers 3 – 4

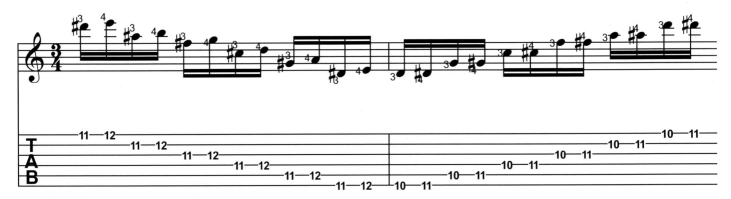

Continue shifting down to the 1st position, then back up to 9th.

Exercise 4: Fingers 4 – 3

Continue shifting down to the 1ˢᵗ position, then back up to 9ᵗʰ.

Slurs

There are a number of slur exercises that you can find in various technique books. They will all benefit you in the long run. Since I'm basing all these exercises on real repertoire, I have chosen to create an exercise that most closely mimics the most difficult conditions we find ourselves in when playing slurs. Many of the most challenging slurs are found with other fingers occupied and locked into position.

Exercise 1: 1ˢᵗ finger fretted, slur with 2 and 4

Exercise 2: 3ʳᵈ finger fretted, slur with 2 and 4

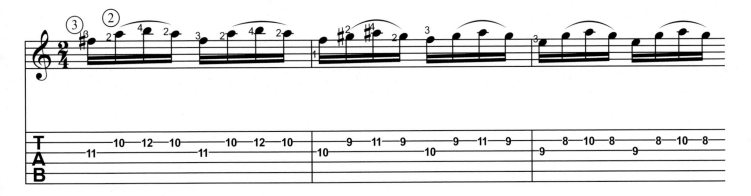

Exercise 3: 1st and 3rd fingers fretted, slur with 2 and 4

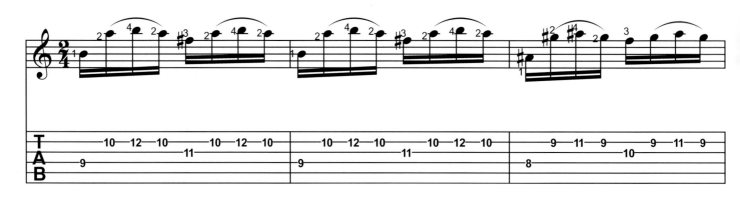

Exercise 4: 2nd finger fretted, slur with 1 and 3

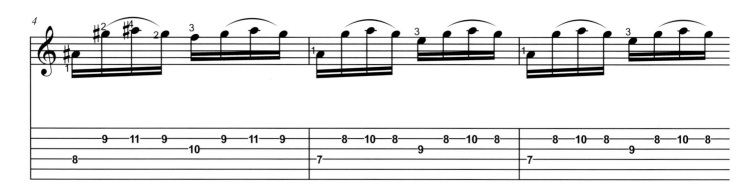

Exercise 5: 4th finger fretted, slur with 1 and 3

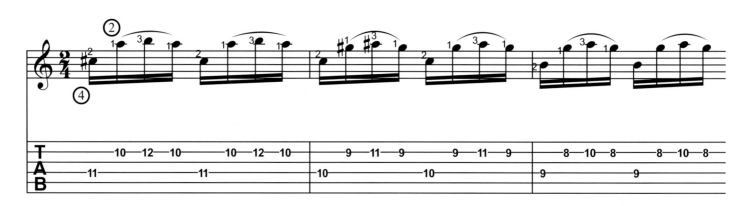

Exercise 6: 2ⁿᵈ and 4ᵗʰ fingers fretted, slur with 1 and 3

Use these as a base and add a level of difficulty by moving the fretted fingers to different strings and increasing the distance between the fretted and slurred strings. E.g. fret on the 5ᵗʰ string and slur on the 2ⁿᵈ string. Also, you can fret with a different finger and use two adjacent fingers to play the slurs.